Only the males have the ruby-colored throat. The throat feathers aren't actually red, though. They look red because of the way they reflect light, like prisms. Sometimes the same feathers look dark, almost black.

The male hummingbird establishes a small territory by chasing other males away. During mating season, when a female visits his territory, he will put on a flying show to impress her. That is what's happening on page 36.

After mating, the female will usually lay two white eggs, each the size of a jellybean. She incubates (sits on the eggs) for eleven to sixteen days until her chicks hatch. The female takes care of the new chicks by herself.

Females can have several broods of chicks in one season. Hummingbirds do not mate for life.

Calliope
Hummingbird

Cardinal
Flower

Anna's
Hummingbird

AAS (American Association for the Advancement of Science)/Subaru Excellence in Children's Books Finalist

Cooperative Children's Book Center Best Book of the Year List

Science magazine's Best Books for Curious Kids

Virginia Readers' Choices

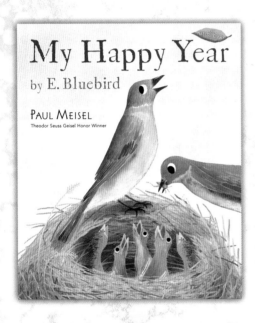

A Junior Library Guild Selection

"A brief, friendly journal-style text accompanied by equally uncluttered and appealing digitally enhanced paintings in sumptuous colors."
—*Horn Book*

A Junior Library Guild Selection

MY TINY LIFE
by Ruby T. Hummingbird

PAUL MEISEL

HOLIDAY HOUSE · NEW YORK

For Andrew and Lauren

Special thanks to Douglas L. Altshuler, Professor in the
Department of Zoology at the University of British Columbia
for his expert review of this book.

Copyright © 2021 by Paul Meisel • All Rights Reserved

HOLIDAY HOUSE is registered in the U.S. Patent and Trademark Office.

Printed and bound in December 2020 at Leo Paper, Heshan, China.

The artwork was created with watercolors, acrylics, and gouache on Arches hot press paper,

and digital tools. • www.holidayhouse.com • First Edition • 1 3 5 7 9 10 8 6 4 2

Library of Congress Cataloging-in-Publication Data

Names: Meisel, Paul, author. • Title: My tiny life by Ruby T. Hummingbird / Paul Meisel. • Description: First edition.

New York City : Holiday House, [2021] | Series: A nature diary | Audience: Ages 4–8 | Audience: Grades K–1 | Summary: "Told in

diary form, My Tiny Life by Ruby T. Hummingbird is an action-packed introduction to the life cycle of a ruby-throated hummingbird"

— Provided by publisher. • Identifiers: LCCN 2020016037 | ISBN 9780823443222 (hardcover) • Subjects: LCSH: Ruby-throated

hummingbird—Juvenile literature. • Classification: LCC QL696.A558 M45 2021 | DDC 598.7/64—dc23

LC record available at https://lccn.loc.gov/2020016037

ISBN: 978-0-8234-4322-2 (hardcover)

MAY 15

Today I poked my way out of this tiny egg.

MAY 16

When I hear wings beating, I open my mouth. Mom feeds me insects and nectar.

MAY 18

I'm already twice as big as I was when I was born.

My feathers are growing.

JUNE 2

Now I'm three times as big as when I was born!
I can beat my wings super-fast like Mom!

JUNE 5

We're walking on the branch where
our nest is. I think my wings are
ready to fly.

ZIP

JUNE 10

I can fly really fast! Up, down, backward, forward!

JUNE 15

I flew fast and caught a bug.

JUNE 17

I found a flower with amazing nectar. So delicious!

JUNE 21

This flower is MINE! No, you don't!

CHASE

BYE!

JUNE 22
What? You're back again?

DOWN

ALL AROUND

JULY 5

ZOOM

Wait! No! TWO of you on MY flower?

20

KICK

CHASE

22

PINCH

WAIT! TIMEOUT!

Fighting is exhausting!
We can share . . . just for today.

AUGUST 22

I'm hearing a lot of chatter about a big trip soon.

SEPTEMBER 4

Eating lots of bugs and drinking lots of nectar.
Getting ready for the big trip.

SEPTEMBER 18

Where are the other hummingbirds? Did they leave?

SEPTEMBER 25

Time to go. I'm off!

OCTOBER 4

Almost there. I'm stopping
for some nectar.

OCTOBER-FEBRUARY

This is a great place to spend the fall and winter. I'm eating lots of bugs and spiders and drinking lots of nectar. But before I know it, I've got to get ready for the big trip home.

Do you like my new red throat? It shows I'm a male.

MARCH 1

5 a.m.
I'm off! Wish me luck!

2 p.m.
Still flying. A short rainstorm,
but there's nowhere to stop.

9 p.m.
I'm getting closer. I have to keep flying
because I'm still over water.

11:30 p.m.
I made it!

MAY 2

I'm home! What a long trip!

MAY 4

I found my flower. And maybe a mate.

GLOSSARY

Archilochus colubris: the scientific name for ruby-throated hummingbird

brood: a family of young birds or other animals born in one hatching

chick: a young, newly hatched bird

incubate: to sit on eggs to keep them warm so the chicks can hatch

migration: when a species, such as hummingbird, moves from regions or habitats because of the change of seasons

nectar: a liquid sugar that plants make and that bees, butterflies, and hummingbirds drink

species: a group of plants or animals that breeds among themselves. Examples of species are common sunflowers, dogs, and humans.

SOURCES AND RECOMMENDED READING

Periodical

James Gorman, "The Hummingbird as Warrior: Evolution of a Fierce and Furious Beak," *New York Times*, February 5, 2019.

Websites

American Bird Conservancy:
https://abcbirds.org/bird/
ruby-throated-hummingbird/

The Cornell Lab:
https://www.allaboutbirds.org/guide/
Ruby-throated_Hummingbird

Audubon:
https://www.audubon.org/field-guide/bird/
ruby-throated-hummingbird

Hummingbirds.net, Species List by State and Province:
http://www.hummingbirds.net/states.html

Hummingbird.net, Ruby-throated Hummingbird:
http://www.hummingbirds.net/rubythroated.html

National Geographic:
https://www.nationalgeographic.com/
animals/birds/r/ruby-throated-hummingbird/

Volunteers who track hummingbird migration

https://journeynorth.org/hummingbirds

Hummingbirds are amazing fliers. They can hover, fly upside down and backward as well as forward at speeds of 30 miles per hour, or 60 miles per hour in a dive. They beat their wings as much as 53 times per second. The hummingbird got its name from the humming sound its wings make.

Hummingbirds have very short legs and aren't terribly good walkers or hoppers. Having short, light legs helps them fly better.

Adult hummingbirds need a lot of food for energy to beat their wings so fast. They can eat as much as half their weight in sugar, or nectar, in one day. They don't suck the nectar through their long bills. Instead, they use a forked tongue to lick it.

Hummingbirds prefer the nectar of orange and red tubular-shaped flowers like trumpet creeper, bee balm, red buckeye, and red morning glory. They also eat tree sap, mosquitoes, gnats, fruit flies, small bees, aphids, caterpillars, and spiders.

Mother hummingbirds feed their chicks a mix of insects and nectar when they are newly hatched because they need protein to grow quickly.

Hummingbirds are good learners. They will return over and over to the same flower or feeder.

Although tiny, hummingbirds are famous for being aggressive and bold. They will attack much larger birds (such as crows, jays and even hawks) that come into their territory. They attack and fight with other hummingbirds as Ruby T. does in this book.

Hummingbird predators include snakes, lizards, bats, jays, crows, ravens, and cats.

Hummingbirds have no sense of smell but excellent eyesight.

The ruby-throated hummingbird only breeds in eastern North America. If the ruby-throated hummingbird doesn't visit your area, you may want to look for Anna's hummingbird or the calliope hummingbird.

Actual Size

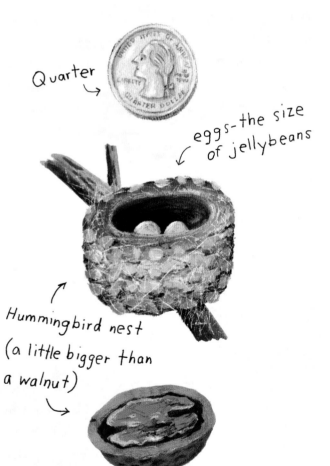

Quarter

eggs—the size of jellybeans

Hummingbird nest (a little bigger than a walnut)